Reasons To Trust America's Mainstream Media

A Comprehensive Guide

By
Richard Maddow

DEDICATION

Dedicated to my BFF, Herman.

RICHARD MADDOW

CONTENTS

REASONS TO TRUST AMERICA'S MAINSTREAM MEDIA

RICHARD MADDOW

ACKNOWLEDGMENTS

I acknowledge inspiration from the fine book
Reasons To Vote For Democrats.
The two books have a lot in common, namely
mostly blank pages, because, for God's sake,
there are few good reasons to vote for Democrats
or to trust the damn Media

.

Chapter One
REASONS TO TRUST CNN
The Complete List

Since the author could find no good reasons, this page has been left mostly blank.

REASONS TO TRUST CNN (CONTINUED)

The Author found no good reasons, so this page
has been left mostly blank.

REASONS TO TRUST CNN (CONTINUED)

The Author found no good reasons, so this page
has been left mostly blank.

REASONS TO TRUST CNN (CONTINUED)

The Author found no good reasons, so this page
has been left mostly blank.

REASONS TO TRUST CNN (CONTINUED)

The Author found no good reasons, so this page
has been left mostly blank.

REASONS TO TRUST CNN (CONTINUED)

The Author found no good reasons, so this page
has been left mostly blank.

REASONS TO TRUST CNN (CONTINUED)

The Author found no good reasons, so this page
has been left mostly blank.

REASONS TO TRUST CNN (CONTINUED)

The Author found no good reasons, so this page
has been left mostly blank.

Chapter 2
REASONS TO TRUST ABC
The Complete List

Since the author could find no good reasons, this page has been left mostly blank.

REASONS TO TRUST ABC (CONTINUED)

The Author found no good reasons, so this page
has been left mostly blank.

REASONS TO TRUST ABC (CONTINUED)

The Author found no good reasons, so this page
has been left mostly blank.

REASONS TO TRUST ABC (CONTINUED)

The Author found no good reasons, so this page
has been left mostly blank.

REASONS TO TRUST ABC (CONTINUED)

The Author found no good reasons, so this page
has been left mostly blank.

RICHARD MADDOW

REASONS TO TRUST ABC (CONTINUED)

The Author found no good reasons, so this page
has been left mostly blank.

REASONS TO TRUST ABC (CONTINUED)

The Author found no good reasons, so this page
has been left mostly blank.

REASONS TO TRUST ABC (CONTINUED)

The Author found no good reasons, so this page
has been left mostly blank.

REASONS TO TRUST ABC (CONTINUED)

The Author found no good reasons, so this page
has been left mostly blank.

REASONS TO TRUST ABC (CONTINUED)

The Author found no good reasons, so this page
has been left mostly blank.

REASONS TO TRUST ABC (CONTINUED)

The Author found no good reasons, so this page
has been left mostly blank.

Chapter 3
REASONS TO TRUST TIME MAGAZINE
The Complete List

Since the author could find no good reasons, this page has been left mostly blank.

REASONS TO TRUST TIME MAGAZINE
(CONTINUED)

The Author found no good reasons, so this page
has been left mostly blank.

REASONS TO TRUST TIME MAGAZINE (CONTINUED)

The Author found no good reasons, so this page has been left mostly blank.

REASONS TO TRUST TIME MAGAZINE
(CONTINUED)

The Author found no good reasons, so this page
has been left mostly blank.

REASONS TO TRUST TIME MAGAZINE (CONTINUED)

The Author found no good reasons, so this page
has been left mostly blank.

REASONS TO TRUST TIME MAGAZINE
(CONTINUED)

The Author found no good reasons, so this page
has been left mostly blank.

REASONS TO TRUST TIME MAGAZINE (CONTINUED)

The Author found no good reasons, so this page
has been left mostly blank.

REASONS TO TRUST TIME MAGAZINE (CONTINUED)

The Author found no good reasons, so this page has been left mostly blank.

REASONS TO TRUST TIME MAGAZINE
(CONTINUED)

The Author found no good reasons, so this page
has been left mostly blank.

Chapter 4
REASONS TO TRUST NBC
The Complete List

Since the author could find no good reasons, this page has been left mostly blank.

REASONS TO TRUST NBC (CONTINUED)

The Author found no good reasons, so this page
has been left mostly blank.

REASONS TO TRUST NBC (CONTINUED)

The Author found no good reasons, so this page
has been left mostly blank.

REASONS TO TRUST NBC (CONTINUED)

The Author found no good reasons, so this page
has been left mostly blank.

REASONS TO TRUST NBC (CONTINUED)

The Author found no good reasons, so this page
has been left mostly blank.

REASONS TO TRUST NBC (CONTINUED)

The Author found no good reasons, so this page
has been left mostly blank.

REASONS TO TRUST NBC (CONTINUED)

The Author found no good reasons, so this page
has been left mostly blank.

REASONS TO TRUST NBC (CONTINUED)

The Author found no good reasons, so this page
has been left mostly blank.

REASONS TO TRUST NBC (CONTINUED)

The Author found no good reasons, so this page
has been left mostly blank.

Chapter 5
REASONS TO TRUST THE WASHINGTON POST
The Complete List

Since the author could find no good reasons, this page has been left mostly blank.

REASONS TO TRUST THE WASHINGTON POST
(CONTINUED)

The Author found no good reasons, so this page
has been left mostly blank.

REASONS TO TRUST THE WASHINGTON POST (CONTINUED)

The Author found no good reasons, so this page
has been left mostly blank.

REASONS TO TRUST THE WASHINGTON POST (CONTINUED)

The Author found no good reasons, so this page
has been left mostly blank.

REASONS TO TRUST THE WASHINGTON POST (CONTINUED)

The Author found no good reasons, so this page
has been left mostly blank.

REASONS TO TRUST THE WASHINGTON POST (CONTINUED)

The Author found no good reasons, so this page
has been left mostly blank.

REASONS TO TRUST THE WASHINGTON POST (CONTINUED)

The Author found no good reasons, so this page
has been left mostly blank.

REASONS TO TRUST THE WASHINGTON POST
(CONTINUED)

The Author found no good reasons, so this page
has been left mostly blank.

REASONS TO TRUST THE WASHINGTON POST (CONTINUED)

The Author found no good reasons, so this page
has been left mostly blank.

REASONS TO TRUST THE WASHINGTON POST (CONTINUED)

The Author found no good reasons, so this page
has been left mostly blank.

REASONS TO TRUST THE WASHINGTON POST (CONTINUED)

The Author found no good reasons, so this page
has been left mostly blank.

REASONS TO TRUST THE WASHINGTON POST (CONTINUED)

The Author found no good reasons, so this page
has been left mostly blank.

REASONS TO TRUST THE WASHINGTON POST (CONTINUED)

The Author found no good reasons, so this page
has been left mostly blank.

REASONS TO TRUST THE WASHINGTON POST (CONTINUED)

The Author found no good reasons, so this page
has been left mostly blank.

REASONS TO TRUST THE WASHINGTON POST (CONTINUED)

The Author found no good reasons, so this page
has been left mostly blank.

REASONS TO TRUST THE WASHINGTON POST (CONTINUED)

The Author found no good reasons, so this page
has been left mostly blank.

Chapter 6
REASONS TO TRUST HUFFINGTON POST
The Complete List

Since the author could find no good reasons, this page has been left mostly blank.

REASONS TO TRUST HUFFINGTON POST (CONTINUED)

The Author found no good reasons, so this page
has been left mostly blank.

REASONS TO TRUST HUFFINGTON POST (CONTINUED)

The Author found no good reasons, so this page
has been left mostly blank.

REASONS TO TRUST HUFFINGTON POST
(CONTINUED)

The Author found no good reasons, so this page
has been left mostly blank.

REASONS TO TRUST HUFFINGTON POST (CONTINUED)

The Author found no good reasons, so this page
has been left mostly blank.

REASONS TO TRUST HUFFINGTON POST (CONTINUED)

The Author found no good reasons, so this page
has been left mostly blank.

REASONS TO TRUST HUFFINGTON POST (CONTINUED)

The Author found no good reasons, so this page
has been left mostly blank.

REASONS TO TRUST HUFFINGTON POST (CONTINUED)

The Author found no good reasons, so this page
has been left mostly blank.

REASONS TO TRUST HUFFINGTON POST (CONTINUED)

The Author found no good reasons, so this page
has been left mostly blank.

REASONS TO TRUST HUFFINGTON POST (CONTINUED)

The Author found no good reasons, so this page
has been left mostly blank.

REASONS TO TRUST HUFFINGTON POST (CONTINUED)

The Author found no good reasons, so this page
has been left mostly blank.

REASONS TO TRUST HUFFINGTON POST (CONTINUED)

The Author found no good reasons, so this page
has been left mostly blank.

REASONS TO TRUST HUFFINGTON POST (CONTINUED)

The Author found no good reasons, so this page
has been left mostly blank.

REASONS TO TRUST HUFFINGTON POST (CONTINUED)

The Author found no good reasons, so this page
has been left mostly blank.

REASONS TO TRUST HUFFINGTON POST (CONTINUED)

The Author found no good reasons, so this page
has been left mostly blank.

Chapter 7
REASONS TO TRUST MSNBC (CONTINUED)
The Complete List

Since the author could find no good reasons, this page has been left mostly blank.

REASONS TO TRUST MSNBC (CONTINUED)

The Author found no good reasons, so this page
has been left mostly blank.

REASONS TO TRUST MSNBC (CONTINUED)

The Author found no good reasons, so this page
has been left mostly blank.

REASONS TO TRUST MSNBC (CONTINUED)

The Author found no good reasons, so this page
has been left mostly blank.

REASONS TO TRUST MSNBC (CONTINUED)

The Author found no good reasons, so this page
has been left mostly blank.

REASONS TO TRUST MSNBC (CONTINUED)

The Author found no good reasons, so this page
has been left mostly blank.

REASONS TO TRUST MSNBC (CONTINUED)

The Author found no good reasons, so this page
has been left mostly blank.

REASONS TO TRUST MSNBC (CONTINUED)

The Author found no good reasons, so this page
has been left mostly blank.

REASONS TO TRUST MSNBC (CONTINUED)

The Author found no good reasons, so this page
has been left mostly blank.

REASONS TO TRUST MSNBC (CONTINUED)

The Author found no good reasons, so this page
has been left mostly blank.

Chapter 8
REASONS TO TRUST THE NEW YORK TIMES
The Complete List

Since the author could find no good reasons, this page has been left mostly blank.

REASONS TO TRUST THE NEW YORK TIMES (CONTINUED)

The Author found no good reasons, so this page
has been left mostly blank.

REASONS TO TRUST THE NEW YORK TIMES
(CONTINUED)

The Author found no good reasons, so this page
has been left mostly blank.

RICHARD MADDOW

REASONS TO TRUST THE NEW YORK TIMES (CONTINUED)

The Author found no good reasons, so this page
has been left mostly blank.

REASONS TO TRUST THE NEW YORK TIMES (CONTINUED)

The Author found no good reasons, so this page
has been left mostly blank.

REASONS TO TRUST THE NEW YORK TIMES (CONTINUED)

The Author found no good reasons, so this page
has been left mostly blank.

REASONS TO TRUST THE NEW YORK TIMES (CONTINUED)

The Author found no good reasons, so this page
has been left mostly blank.

RICHARD MADDOW

REASONS TO TRUST THE NEW YORK TIMES (CONTINUED)

The Author found no good reasons, so this page
has been left mostly blank.

Chapter 9
REASONS TO TRUST NPR
The Complete List

Since the author could find no good reasons, this page has been left
mostly blank.

REASONS TO TRUST NPR (CONTINUED)

The Author found no good reasons, so this page
has been left mostly blank.

REASONS TO TRUST NPR (CONTINUED)

The Author found no good reasons, so this page
has been left mostly blank.

RICHARD MADDOW

REASONS TO TRUST NPR (CONTINUED)

The Author found no good reasons, so this page
has been left mostly blank.

REASONS TO TRUST NPR (CONTINUED)

The Author found no good reasons, so this page
has been left mostly blank.

REASONS TO TRUST NPR (CONTINUED)

The Author found no good reasons, so this page
has been left mostly blank.

REASONS TO TRUST NPR (CONTINUED)

The Author found no good reasons, so this page
has been left mostly blank.

Chapter 10
REASONS TO TRUST CBS
The Complete List

Since the author could find no good reasons, this page has been left mostly blank.

REASONS TO TRUST CBS (CONTINUED)

The Author found no good reasons, so this page
has been left mostly blank.

REASONS TO TRUST CBS (CONTINUED)

The Author found no good reasons, so this page
has been left mostly blank.

REASONS TO TRUST CBS (CONTINUED)

The Author found no good reasons, so this page
has been left mostly blank.

REASONS TO TRUST CBS (CONTINUED)

The Author found no good reasons, so this page
has been left mostly blank.

REASONS TO TRUST CBS (CONTINUED)

The Author found no good reasons, so this page
has been left mostly blank.

REASONS TO TRUST CBS (CONTINUED)

The Author found no good reasons, so this page
has been left mostly blank.

REASONS TO TRUST CBS (CONTINUED)

The Author found no good reasons, so this page
has been left mostly blank.

Chapter 11
REASONS TO TRUST THE NEW YORKER
The Complete List

Since the author could find no good reasons, this page has been left mostly blank.

REASONS TO TRUST THE NEW YORKER (CONTINUED)

The Author found no good reasons, so this page
has been left mostly blank.

REASONS TO TRUST THE NEW YORKER
(CONTINUED)

The Author found no good reasons, so this page
has been left mostly blank.

REASONS TO TRUST THE NEW YORKER (CONTINUED)

The Author found no good reasons, so this page
has been left mostly blank.

REASONS TO TRUST THE NEW YORKER
(CONTINUED)

The Author found no good reasons, so this page
has been left mostly blank.

Bonus Chapter
REASONS TO TRUST FOX NEWS

According to a new poll, in the question of which national news outlet is the most trusted, Fox News comes out on top.

20 percent said they trust Fox News' coverage "a great deal," compared to 14 percent each for NBC, CBS, and ABC, MSNBC's 11 percent, and 18 percent for CNN.

To save your valuable time, I'll just summarize the reasons to trust Fox News: Fox News is simply MORE TRUSTWORTHY IN EVERY WAY.

ABOUT THE AUTHOR

Before becoming a full-time author, Richard Maddow worked as a Lifeguard at a nudist beach in Mexico, a telephone Psychic and a Skyscraper Window Washer at Trump Tower, NY.